ABB AS, Robotics
P.O Box 265,
N-4349 Bryne, Norway
Tel.: +47 51 48 90 00
Fax: +47 51 48 37 25

Rogaland has most of what makes Norway a polished diamond
among the world's holiday destinations. The landscape is like
the backdrop to a fairy-tale; flat or sheer, it is rich in contrasts,
and the constantly changing weather is like the curtain separating
the different acts of the play. Like the drama of life itself,
it is sometimes romantic, with mild breezes and colourful sunsets,
sometimes stormy and sensational.
At these latitudes, there should be snow and ice all year round, but
we can thank the Gulf Stream for the exciting climate we have.

Come on a voyage into our often spectacular scenery, with eternal
snow and ice on the highest peaks, a few miles away green pastures
year round. To the deep and wild fjords, to the flat, wind-scoured
Jæren, and the ocean that thunders alongside.
Or to the skerries and the sheltered inshore basin, full of islands
and narrow sounds - an Eldorado for yachtsmen and fishermen.
Or how about a hunt for our ancestors, for traces of the first
immigrants of the Stone Age? Walk in wonder and reflection -
what has happened here, how was the land formed, what did they
do? Rogaland is a huge museum of natural and cultural history.

This book is organised as a voyage, a hunt for natural attractions
and experiences.

Snorre Aske

Natur og Kulturforlaget A.S

Natur og Kulturforlaget A.S. 1997, N-4440 Tonstad, Norway. Tel. +47 38 370 350 / +47 51 881 997.
Design: Arnøy Sats & Repro A.S. Pre-press: Reprobanen A.S. Print: Aske Trykkeri A.S. Binding: Bokbinderiet Johnsen A.S.

NORWAY

Rogaland in Norway
- between the ocean and the fjords

Stavanger harbour

Our towns and cities are based on natural resources. The most obvious of these is fish, we had unbelievable quantities in the sea, particularly herring. It is said that Haugesund was built on herring-bones. For reasons we do not understand, the herring disappeared in the 1880s, and this whole epoch ended in tears, bankruptcies galore. But our bountiful nature gave us a new gift: in the deep fjords we found the brisling, or the sardine as it is called after canning. A new boom began, and in one way or another most of the population was involved with this little fish. However, nature always goes in waves, and in the 1960s this epoch also came to an end, facing us with very hard times. Yet again salvation came from the sea - the oil age. Thanks to its location, and the initiative of some very able people, Stavanger was chosen to be Norway's oil capital. The city is in constant change, but old buildings are well-preserved; Old Stavanger, one of our "white towns", is a living and very pleasant residential community.

Stavanger became a bishopric in the 1120s, and the Cathedral was begun. It was nearly destroyed in the great fire of 1272, but was repaired and extended; as a result the nave is Romanesque (Norman) and the choir is Gothic.

Alexander Kielland

Stavanger harbour

6

Gamle (old) Stavanger.   Stavanger Cathedral   Gamle (old) Stavanger.

Engøyholmen.

Skagen brygge (quay), Stavanger.

The Bynuten peak.

SANDNES - THE CYCLE TOWN IN THE COUNTRYSIDE

Sandnes is situated where the mountains and fjords of Ryfylke meet the flat coastal strip of Jæren. When the ice receded after the last ice age, much of what is now the municipality of Sandnes was covered by clay, sand and gravel. The clay subsequently became the raw material for industries - the manufacture of tiles and pottery. Today the town is better known for its textile and cycle industry - it likes to call itself the cycle town. Cycles have been made here for almost a hundred years. You can borrow a bike free of charge and ride through beautiful and interesting surroundings.

This is the place for outdoor enthusiasts - there are few places in Norway offering so much variety. There is ample opportunity for the keen angler - both in the sea and in lakes. The Figgjo river is famous for its good salmon and trout fishing, with fish up to 10-15 kilos. We can also recommend a canoe trip along the Lutsi watercourse. Long waterways alternating between open waters and narrow sounds, offering exciting experiences and challenges for everyone. The Bynuten peak is also an enticing destination, affording a panoramic view of the mountains and deep fjords of Ryfylke. And, if you turn around, you will see the flat Jæren landscape and the sea - giving you a good impression of the contrasts of our countryside. Norway's biggest arboretum is situated at Melsheia - idyllic, family-friendly paths wind among Scandinavian and more exotic bushes and trees from many parts of the world. If you are surprised by bad weather, you can seek refuge in Norway's biggest indoor "waterland" - "Havanna".

On the way to the Dalsnuten peak, with view of the Gandsfjord and Sandnes.

Gandsfjord, "construction yard" for oil platforms.

Salmon fishing in the Figgjo river.

There are miles and miles of pleasant cycle tracks in Sandnes.

The Lutsi lake, the wilds in the town.

From the petroglyph field
on Åmøy island.

Ancient Monuments

This was the first region of Norway to emerge from the ice, and so the first to be settled - hunters moved up from the south about 12,000 years ago. The whole area is full of ancient monuments, like an open-air museum. If we look at the tools and ornaments they left, we can see that these were clever hunters and craftsmen. It almost beggars belief that a fishhook can be made of flint, and that you can actually catch fish with it - but we can see from the petroglyphs that they caught big fish like halibut with this tackle. From the jewellery we can see that our ancestors were inordinately vain and by no means as primitive as we sometimes think.

The Norsemen are the only people who have named a weekday after washing - the modern lørdag (Saturday) is from laugardag, washday. That they had the time to develop such a high culture must have been because the land was in many ways a generous one.

1. Landa, an ancient village at Forsand.
2. The stone cross from Kvitsøy dates from the Early Middle Ages.
3. Bronze horns from the Early Bronze Age. Revheim.
4. Flint dagger, Bø, Karmøy.
5. The Iron Age farm at Ullandhaug has been reconstructed on ancient farm-house foundations going back 14-15 centruries. In the summer there are activities here showing daily life at that time.

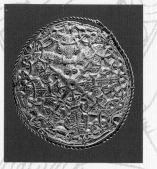

Buckle from Nedrabø in Bokn

The Swords in the Stone
monument by Frits Røed
symbolises the battle.

The battle of Hafrsfjord

It was here the decisive sea-battle to unify Norway was fought in 872.

Harald Fairhair defeated the local chieftains, took the title of king and ruled
for the rest of his long life from Avaldsnes on the island of Karmøy.
A Viking ship is a work of art, a perfect mixture of functionality and aesthetics.
Amazing that they could be built with such primitive tools.
These ships flew over the water like swans, totally superior to the vessels of contemporary
cultures; the Vikings ruled the seas for 200 years.

The fjords

The fjords and the surrounding areas were perfect Viking lairs. For this trading and hunting people, the fjords corresponded to our road network; their fast vessels made short work of the distance between the mountain realm and the open ocean. The steep-sided fjords were also good hiding-places, and it was easy to spot unwanted guests approaching: people thought twice about sailing into such natural traps. Rich hunting and fishing were the prime incentives to settle here, and in the winter the best place was the edge of the ocean, where the Gulf Stream kept the icebergs away and seal and whale could be hunted. In the spring, however, when the snows melted, people moved inland and up into the mountains to exploit the upland resources, such as the great reindeer herds. The early Norwegians were thus nomads, moving home with the seasons.

Kayakers enjoying a more intense experience of Nature.

Jøsenfjord.

12

There are large stocks of seal in the fjord.

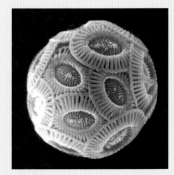

Emiliana Huxleyi

Why is the fjord green?

Sometimes the fjord turns a greenish colour, a strange phenomenon that can have two different causes. One of them is an algae called Emiliania huxleyi. In itself it is not green, but rather a golden brown, and to increase the confusion it is covered with white chalk flakes; but it reflects the light through the water and so turns the fjord green. The other cause is the meltwater from glaciers and snowfields, which carries suspended silicates that also reflect the light in a special way.

Algae season in Lysefjorden.

Mountains and waterfalls

Lysefjord is probably one of the world's wildest fjords. Here the mountains rise vertically out of the water, sometimes to 1000 metres. When the boat creeps up to the rock walls, which in many places overhang, you feel small. Beneath the keel is another 450 metres - of water. Strange to think that it is ice and gravel that have excavated these enormous formations.

Right: Månafossen. Is there a pot of gold at the end of this rainbow? In winter the falls can build a castle of ice.

Left: Waterfall in Lysefjorden.

Cold and pure water.

14

Pulpit Rock

- Hanging over us, 600
metres up.
This is the undisputed
number-one natural tourist
attraction hereabouts.
There is a deep crack behind
this rock formation,
constantly widened by
melting and refreezing.
If and when Pulpit Rock falls
into the fjord, it will be a
catastrophe - there will be
a giant wave scouring the
fjordsides for miles in both
directions.

Eagle. Golden eagles from
other parts of Scandinavia
come to the southerly districts
of Rogaland for the winter.

Panorama

Pulpit Rock is a two-hour hike through the Norwegian wilderness. Some people find it a tough trip, but they are rewarded for their toil and tears with a fabulous view, a lifetime memory. Far beneath us, Lysefjord curls like a sleeping dragon for 40 km. When you are once up here, spend the whole day; walk along the edge of the fjord and soak up the exciting views. The weather can change very rapidly, everything looks different as the light varies, and no two days are alike. It is a special experience to spend the night here in your sleeping-bag, with Pulpit Rock all to yourself. Look at the preceding page for an early morning mood, the first rays of the sun reflected in the fjord.

Preikestolhytta mountain lodge, the starting-point for the trip.

Intrepid explorers will find the Needle about 2 km west of Pulpit Rock.

Morning light at Preikestolen.

Winter mood.

A quiet spot

Sandwiched between the huge, rugged mountains are small green oases, in some of which people made their homes. For large parts of the year they see no sun, but in high summer they develop a very warm microclimate; the mountains radiate the heat after the sun goes down. In many places the only access was by ladder up the steepest part, a ladder which could be removed when the taxman or sheriff came calling.

Right: Lysefjorden.

Here you have the mountains at close quarters.

Bakken farm, far from the madding crowd.

Kjerag

Further up the fjord the mountain walls rise even higher. We have now reached the mighty massif of Kjerag, 1000 vertical metres above us. This is the Eldorado of the BASE jumpers, who come on pilgrimage from all over the world to jump off Kjerag. The high mountain dropping sheer into the fjord is unique, there is nowhere else in the world like it.

Ørnesvingene

After Kjerag comes Ørnesvingene, the Eagle's Bends, one of Norway's most dramatic roads. The lower part twists in spirals inside the mountain, then in 27 hairpin bends to about 1000 metres above sea level. Here are the summer pastures of Øygardstølen (or Ørneredet, the Eagle's Nest), with a panoramic view of Lysefjorden and Lysebotnen.

The cottar's son from Lysefjorden who wanted to walk to America

Once upon a time in Lysefjorden there was a strange man called Ole Olsen Sognesand. He was called Pilt-Ola, or Ola the Gimp, because of a limp he had from a shipboard accident in his youth.

From poverty in the isolated Lysefjorden, he rose on the back of imaginative new ideas to a business empire. At that time there were incredible quantities of herring in the sea, which was salted down in wooden barrels. Ola invented a revolutionary new salting method, in large watertight seahouses.
In seasons with a lot of fish the barrel supply could be a bottleneck, and then Ola the Gimp could take large quantities of herring and salt them anyway. This made him the richest man in the region, owing much land and three churches. An upstart is never universally popular, of course; and what goes up, must come down. He was convicted of supplying rotten fish - unjustly so, the man's real crime was being a hundred years ahead of his time. After a long series of lawsuits he went spectacularly bankrupt.

This legendary figure was not so easily broken, however. In those days farmers had to make use of anything green their animals could eat. In the summer they swung the scythe at every tuft, and as the snow retreated and the grass grew, they trudged wearily across the mountains looking for fodder, which in the winter they brought back on sledges.
In his long days in the mountains Ola the Gimp had often encountered wild reindeer, Norway's first immigrant and a very frugal animal. Another bright idea came to him: why not tame them? The reindeer could find their own food in the mountains, and come to be butchered on their own steam. This time he had the backing of the venerable Royal Norwegian Society for Rural Development. Ola the Gimp walked all the way to Northern Sweden and Finland, bought up reindeer and drove them back to the Lyse moors. However, he lost a large proportion of his herd in Setesdalen, and the whole fantastic idea ended up in another bankruptcy.

One of his wildest ideas was his attempt to walk to America. Norway was experiencing hard times, and in 1825 Cleng Peerson was fitting out the first emigration ship "SS Restauration" for the Atlantic crossing. Ola the Gimp, however, set his face in the opposite direction and went for a little stroll through Norway, Sweden, Finland, Russia and Siberia, heading for the Bering Strait and Alaska. He never made it, was away for 17 years, and returned a much changed man. But he was just as full of ideas as ever, and achieved many impressive things. He became a living legend, inspiration for a thousand stories.

Ola the Gimp is the quintessential Rogalending: hard-working, full of ideas and initiative, plenty of guts, a visionary.

Ola the Gimp's route across Siberia. Illustration: Svein Magnus Håvardstein.

The hiking culture, a Norwegian heritage?

Norwegians are strange creatures: as soon as it gets warm and springlike along the coast, we get itchy feet and run up into the mountains, back to the snow. As if we hadn't had enough of it during the long winter! Many foreigners have surely scratched their heads over this. Here is a logical explanation. As children we were taken on trips in the forest and mountains, as our parents were before us. This began with our ancestors' nomadic wanderings from fjord to mountain, looking for food. Nowadays it's not the food that's important, but the experience of nature, one which we want to share with our children. And so it goes on, from generation to generation. The whole business of mountain and forest hiking is found most in societies that kept transhumance and hunting longest, given that the topographical conditions are also right.

Between heaven and earth

The hike to Kjerag is one of the most spectacular and dramatic you can have, but definitely not for acrophobics. It can take a while for the stomach to get used to so much empty space below. Walking along the edge is like being on the wing of a plane - watch your step! This is also the realm of the wild reindeer.

The Kjerag Nose watching over Lysefjorden like a sphinx. Notice the cracks in the rock that sketch a mysterious smile.

The Kjeragjuvet ravine. Above the clouds is always the sun.

Mountain holiday

It is a free life up here in the mountains, there is no better relaxation. Here is peace for body and soul, and a recharging of batteries. Match the rhythm of the animals, rise at dawn - that's when it all happens in nature! In the middle of the day the animals take a rest, and so can you. On a warm day it is wonderful to stretch out in the heather, breathe the fresh mountain air and take a nap. The special atmosphere of evening, what we call the Blue Hour, must be experienced with all senses wide open. A day that is divided up in this way lasts longer.

40

Mælen in Suldal.

"The mountain sheep are sweeter".....

In the mountains the grazing plants contain up to three times as much protein as those in the lowlands. Grass and the various herbs are food for many animals, and sheep are among the competitors.
As soon as the snow melts in the spring, the sheep and their lambs are let out to wander the mountains, looking for the best places that they remember from the year before. Throughout the summer they fatten on this wonderful natural pasture and the pure water. In the autumn they are ingathered by the shepherds with their dogs and driven homewards in flocks thousands strong. This is quite a sight, and when they get to the farm there is a big party. The good upland pasture gives the meat a high quality and a rich taste. Norway has many special culinary traditions.
One delicacy is barbequed lamb heads or feet.

Gathering the sheep.

Røynevarden, Suldalsvatnet.

Sirekrok, Sirdal.

Nature is the home of culture.

We harvest what Nature gives us - berries, mushrooms, fish and game. This is why the first Norwegians came here, this is our heritage and our culture. Not picking the berries won't make there be more next year, and it is the same with fish and game. Nature has her own balance, and does not tolerate too many individuals of the same species; the surplus has to die back. And it is the surplus that we must gather. As we become urbanised, we lose touch with nature. When people hate all hunting on principle, it can only be due to remoteness from nature and lack of understanding of the original way of life.

Smoking of reindeer hams.

Sun-drying trout.

Storehouse, Roalkvam in Suldal.

A successful moose hunt.

National Highway 520 between Sauda and Røldal is closed for the winter.

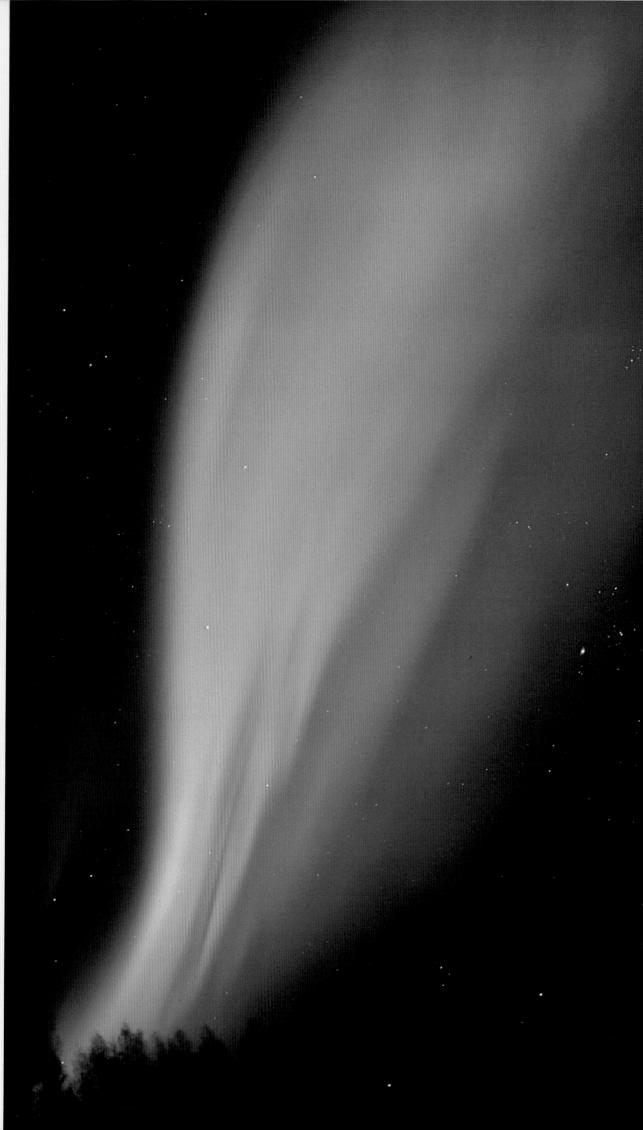

Starry sky and the Northern Lights

In the mountains the sky is closer. Get away from the dust and lights of the city and you will see a starry sky in a new and more intense way. Everyone should have the experience of sitting a night out by a little fire, soaking up the sounds and moods of the night, letting the mystery and phenomena of the sky penetrate their souls. Perhaps we will catch a glimpse of the primeval in us. If you are particularly lucky you may see the Northern Lights.

The Northern Lights. There are many stories about these, and one is about swans which flew too far north and froze to the ice. The flames of the Lights are the beating of their wings to get free.

Stone Age settlement

Helleren, with its natural rock ceiling, has been a shelter since the Stone Age. A fisherman later built his house under it. He did not need to use tiles, as the overhanging rock keeps the rain off.

Feda in Kvinesdal.

A hop, skip and jump, and here we are in Jæren. From soaring mountains and boulderfields to the flat plain of Jæren with its ploughed fields and flowery pastures is no great distance. This is an impressive experience, even for the frequent visitor. The constantly changing weather, with sun, rain and fog in all four seasons, means that the trip is never the same twice.

The story of Gloppedalsura.

Two farms lie buried under the great boulderfield of Gloppe-dalsura. The story goes that the people of these farms were unchristian folk, terrible drinkers and brawlers.

To punish them for the sins and deviltry, God sent a dreadful storm with thunder and lightening, stronger than anyone had ever experienced before. The lightning hamme-red without cease at the steep mountainsides, each time worse than the last. It was like the Day of Judgement. Finally, in a flash like the splitting of the firmament itself, the lightning struck both sides of the valley at the same time; it was too much for the old mountains, and the whole cliffs gave way. Both farms were buried by gigantic landslides, and not a mouse escaped.

Geologists tell us that the river that came from Hunnedalen originally ran westwards here, but now turns to reach the sea at Dirdal.

It is also said that one of the farms had a cock that crowed madly. He was in the grain-bin at the time, survived the landslide with lots to eat but couldn't get out: for many years people could hear sinister crowing from the rocks.

Gloppedalsura is now one of the world's biggest boulder-fields.

The Russian barque Kruzenshtern passing the Eigerøy lighthouse.

EGERSUND - NORWAY'S BIGGEST FISH RECEIVING STATION

With its strategic and sheltered position, along an otherwise wild and exposed coastline, Egersund has always been a natural venue for seafarers.

The small wooden houses remind us of times gone by, when proud sailing ships were also part of the scene. People seem to have more time for each other and life is more relaxed than in the city.

With its proximity to rich fishing grounds and the North Sea as its nearest neighbour, Egersund has become Norway's biggest fish receiving station.

For outdoor pursuits enthusiasts there are all types of hunting and fishing. Trout in the lakes and salmon in the rivers - and plenty of good sea angling for the less patient. You will not have to wait long for your first bite.

The coastal scenery here is wild and beautiful - perhaps even more beautiful and exciting under the sea than on land? Diving conditions are among the best in Europe. The biological diversity is unique - with large forests of seaweed down to a depth of 30 metres - and a multitude of wrecks along the coast.

Egersund harbour- a visit from the past.

Eigerøy lighthouse - with sea-sculpted landscape.

Still coastal waters, sheltered from the ocean.

The fishing port on a festive day.

Find peace and quiet in Egersund.

Eigerøy lighthouse.

The UNESCO-protected Terland footbridge.

Stone walls and wind-bent trees

Jæren is at the north-east corner of the North Sea, and has a climate and fertile soil that few other places on our coast can match.

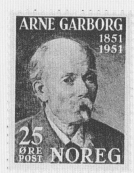

The writer Arne Garborg was born in Jæren and lived much of his life here. His writings contain the fruit of quiet meditation.

Money.

"Money can buy you everything, they say. No you can't.

*You can buy food,
but not appetite,
pills but not health,
soft beds but not sleep,
learning but not sense,
ostentation but not friendship,
servants but not loyalty,
grey hair but not honour,
quiet days but not peace.*

Money can buy you the shell of everything, but not the meat - it's not for sale."

This is Norway's larder, and the farmers are renowned for being capable and industrious. The coast is also a port of call for migratory birds flying between the Arctic and Southern Europe. They enjoy a good rest after the ocean crossing, and find lots of food on the beaches and in the shallow lakes. The flat landscape is dominated by its stone walls. The odd tree may take root behind a wall, but as soon as it rises above its shelter it gets bent and twisted by the dominant westerly wind. Many a Jæren farmer's back has been broken by the effort of clearing all the stones out of the fields and into the walls, but he has left a lasting monument to his toil.

Orrevannet lake.

Ræve on Jæren.

Børaunen, Randaberg.

Jæren is the fruit of the fjords

When the ice excavated the fjords it had to put the debris somewhere. Think of Lysefjorden, with 1000 metres above and 450 metres below the present waterline - the missing mass is now the plains of Jæren, together with material brought over even longer distances.

From the fjords to the flat Jæren in such a short distance is an incredible contrast. Nowhere else in Norway has so long and fine beaches.

Sele, Jæren.

Nærland beach.

Friends at Orrestranden.

The beach at Sola.

Round boulders and erratics

When storms send big waves onto this shore, you can hear a powerful rumbling from this beach. Rocks are thrown up the beach and roll back down again, rubbing each other round. In time they get smaller and smaller, and the upshot is long sandy beaches. It is fascinating to study the shapes and colours of the rocks. A red stone may have been carried by the ice all the way from the Oslo area, while a green one may have come from Suldal in northern Rogaland. Any flint you find is probably Danish. The round stones have always been highly-valued building materials - they last forever and need neither paint nor maintenance. Børaunen.

Picture: Boathouse at Bø in Randaberg.

The boulder beach Børaunen, Randaberg.

Utstein Abbey

Norway's best-preserved monastery was founded by King Magnus Lawmender in the 13th century. This was also one of Harald Fairhair's most important royal seats, chosen with acute sense of strategic location. Here, at the tip of Mosterøy island, you are right in the middle of the coastal channel, and from the high cliffs it is easy to observe both ships and burning beacons. A perfect eyrie for a Viking king. There is said to be a ghost here, a lady in white.

Feistein Light.

Tungenes Light.

Fjøløy Light.

The skerries

Jæren is open to the ocean and unprotected, but the rest of the coast is generally screened by islands and skerries. Here there are many sheltered harbours for fishermen, with space for a homestead and a field or two. Outside the door is the infinite ocean, offering food with one hand and death with the other. Churchyards in such areas are dominated by women's names, for their men are lost at sea.

The puffin nests on the outermost rocks

View from Kvitsøy

Halibut

Moonfish

Linge and skate

Angler fish

The skerry archipelago. Oystercatcher sheltering from the storm, skerries at the edge of the ocean.

Boiling prawns

Prawn trawler

Lobster

Skjæravika, Kvitsøy.

A yachtsman's paradise

Ryfylke is a fantastic region for cabin-dwellers and yachtsmen. Here you can fish to your heart's content. It is quite an experience to catch crabs on the slabby rocks in the middle of the night, then go ashore on an islet and make a meal fit for a king. Crabs should be cooked and eaten on the spot, with the one you most love! Sit by the fire a summer's night and wait for the dawn, when the seabirds start their day.

The heathlands dominate the westerly part of Northern Rogaland. In late summer it is wonderful to see the heather flower and the bees hurrying back and forth over the landscape. On hot days you can actually smell the honey!

Main picture: Tananger

This picture is from Bokn.

Riskafjord.   Proud angler.   Rennesøy

The Danish schooner "Den Store Bjørn" (The Great Bear) in the Skudefjord.

THE WHITE TOWN - SKUDENESHAVN.

Right on the southern tip of the island of Karmøy is the charming sailing-ship town of Skudeneshavn. It would be hard to find a more beautiful harbour. The town was a centre for seafarers in western Norway in the eighteenth and nineteenth centuries, when the fishing was really good. The sea was literally teeming with herring and people flocked to join the party - and to earn money!

Most of the town is preserved as it was, in Empire style, with white painted houses and red-tiled roofs.

We can recommend a walk through the narrow streets, with the sheltered, fertile patches of garden - The atmosphere has not changed much in the last 150 years. You might take the time to chat with the locals, who are proud of their town.

It is not surprising that this town has won a prize as one of Norway's best preserved wood-en towns.

The harbour is a very good starting point for sea-angling trips and you are guaranteed a catch.

Morning mood on the sea.

Well-kept idyllic spots.

There's fish in the sea!

The first man to the fishing field. There is an active sea-fishing club on Karmøy. The club organises regular international sea-fishing festivals attracting anglers from all over the world - all after the big fish.

Old Skudenes has a well-kept and old-world charm.

Yet another breath of times gone by. Participants in the Cutty Sark Tall Ships Race, racing on the Skudefjord.

Attractive white wooden houses with red tiles from Sandnes dominate the Skudenes townscape.

The Visnes copper mines - "birthplace" of the Statue of Liberty in New York. All the copper ore used for this gigantic work of art came from these mines.

NOR-WAY, way to the North - KARMSUNDET

The Karmsund sound - also called the old King's Road - had another name: the way to the North - "Noreg" - "Norway" - a name now used for the whole nation.

The King's farm at Avaldnes was Norway's first "capital". The royal power was based on control of the Karmsund sound. The waters on the outer side of Karmøy island are turbulent and dangerous, forcing traffic to take the route between the island and the mainland. For centuries before the Viking Age, this was the seat of a mighty chieftain who controlled sea traffic and trade along the whole of the Norwegian coast. At the battle of Hafrsfjord Harald Fairhair defeated his opponents, and took up residence at Avaldsnes, from where he ruled his newly united kingdom. There is an active group of historically interested people on Karmøy island and a Viking festival is organised every year. A reconstructed Viking farm is being erected on Bukkøy, near to St Olav's church.

Evening mood by the ocean.

Killer whales in Karmsund sound, with St Olav's church at Avaldnes in the background.

Tonjer lighthouse, seen from the national monument at Haraldshaugen.

The "blue hour" by the sea.

St Olav's church, built in 1250.　　　Copy of Viking ship.　　　You can almost smell the tar.

The Viking festival is organised every year on Karmøy island.

Norway's national monument at Haraldshaugen.

HAUGESUND - THE TOWN THAT LOVES FESTIVALS

The "herring town" of Haugesund - facing the North Sea - with islands, coastal waters, fjords, waterfalls and snow-clad mountains. There is a feeling of history about the place. According to Snorre, the writer of sagas, Harald Fairhair was buried at Haraldshaugen, now the site of a national monument erected in 1872, a thousand years after Harald united Norway.

The monument is a large stone pillar, encircled by 29 smaller stone pillars, symbolising each of the counties Harald united under his rule.

Festive things are always happening in Haugesund.

Film festival, fishing festival, the "Sildajazz" jazz festival, the "Amanda run, harbour days, folk dance gathering, the world's longest herring buffet.

One event is followed by another. People flock to the town from near and far. Smedasundet, the town's most important "street", fills up with visiting boats - you can almost cross the sound dry-shod. Haugesund offers a real folk festival - it's a pleasure to visit. There is something warm, pleasant and welcoming about the people here.

The town's most important "street" is the Smedasund sound.

The world's longest herring buffet.

The Haugesund arms - three seagulls.

"Harbour days".

City feeling - evening mood from bridge over the Karmsund sound.

Sildajazz

This lady has her roots in Haugesund.

Our Saviour's church

Haugesund by night.

Feistein Light in the western ocean.

The divers´ paradise

The west coast of Norway is the most exciting place in Europe for a diver, thanks to its unique biodiversity.

1. Hermit crab and sea anemone.
2. Catfish.
3. Brill roe.
4. Lobster.
5. Lithodes.
6. Angler fish (or monkfish).
7. Plaice.
8. Catfish.
9. Sea anemone og crab.
10. Sea urchin.
11. Sea urchin.
12. Sea-slug.
13. Seapens.
14. Jellyfish.
15. Sea-slug on widgeon grass.
16. Sea anemone.´
17. Squid.
18. Sea anemone.
19. Colony of sea squirts.

Lysebo
Ørnesving
Sauda
Jøsenfjorden
Årdal
Nesvik
Hjelmeland
Jelsa
Ombo
Vikedal
Nedstrand
Finnøy
Ølen
Sandeid
Rennes
Kårstø
Utstein Klost
Mosterøy
Bokn
Kopervik
Haugesund
Karmøy
Skudesneshavi

Photographs

Arvid Tjøstheim: Title page, p.12top.R, p.23, p.43top. p.52-53 R.
Archaeological Museum, Stavanger: p.9. p.70top.L.
Hildegard Håheim: Rosemaling p.4.
Harry Båtsvik, Universy of Bergen: p.13top.R.
Jan Arve Dale: p.14top.L.

Urpo Tarnanen: p.15, p.17R., p.40m., p.44B.L., p.49top.R., p.57B
Magne K. Tjøstheim: p.14R., p.19B.R., p.27.
Johannes Jenson: p.16 top.L.
Odd Inge Worsøe: p.24.B.R.
Ole A. Knutsen: p.26.
Husmo Foto as: p.57R.